Para
Patricio:
Espero que le guste
estos poemas de
cariño, la luz que
ilumina el mundo
Saludos:
Francisco X. Alarcón
6 de mayo 2011

DE AMOR OSCURO

OF DARK LOVE

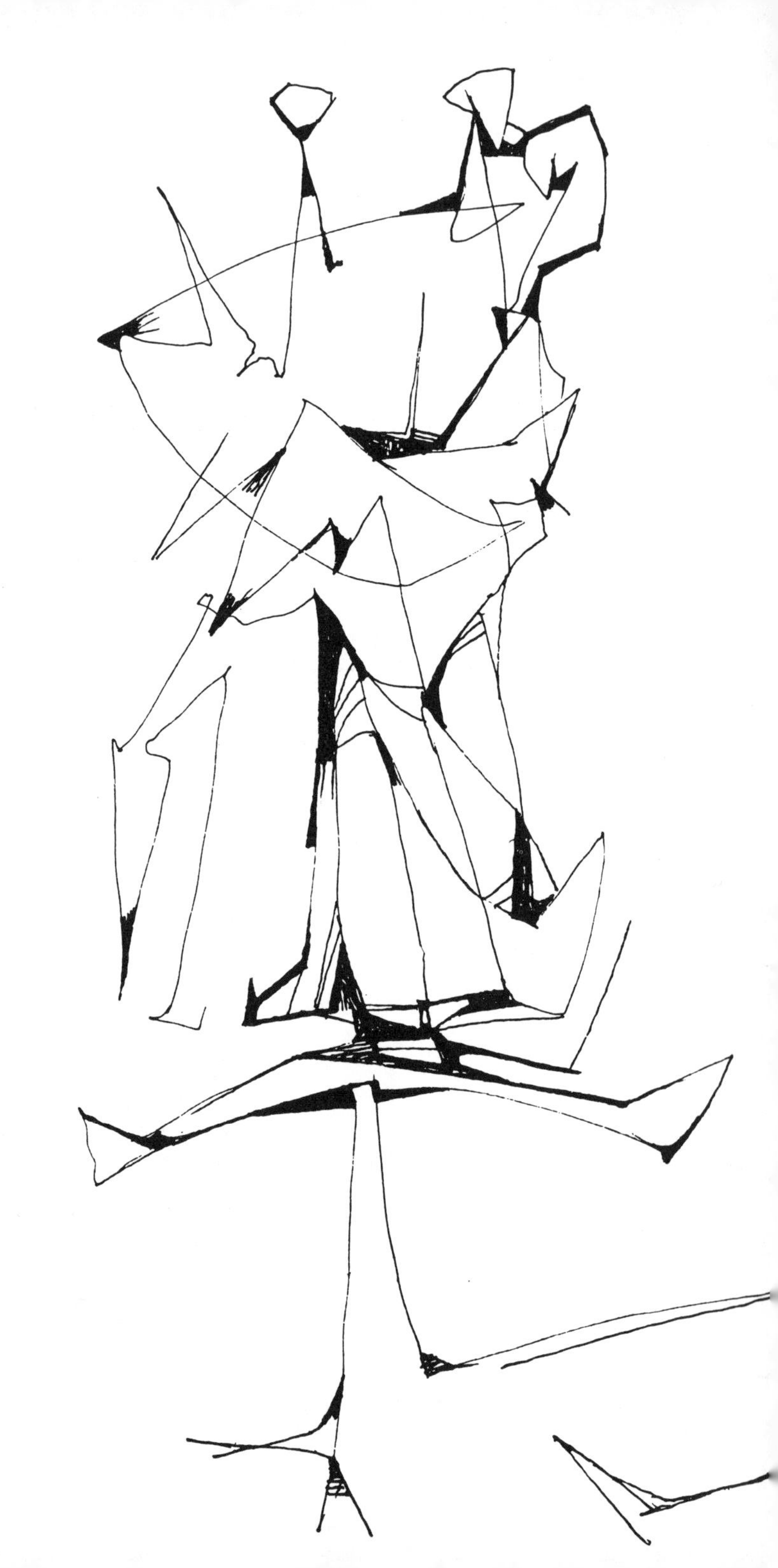

Francisco X. Alarcón

DE AMOR OSCURO

English translation by Francisco Aragon
Drawings by Ray Rice

OF DARK LOVE

Moving Parts Press

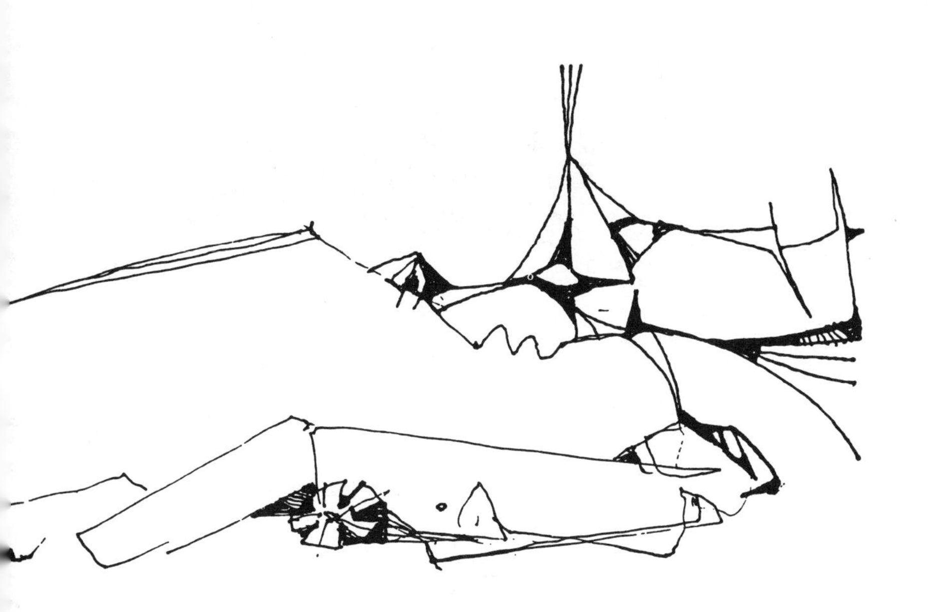

English translation by Francisco Aragon with the poet.

Special thanks to Adrienne Rich
for early translations of some poems.

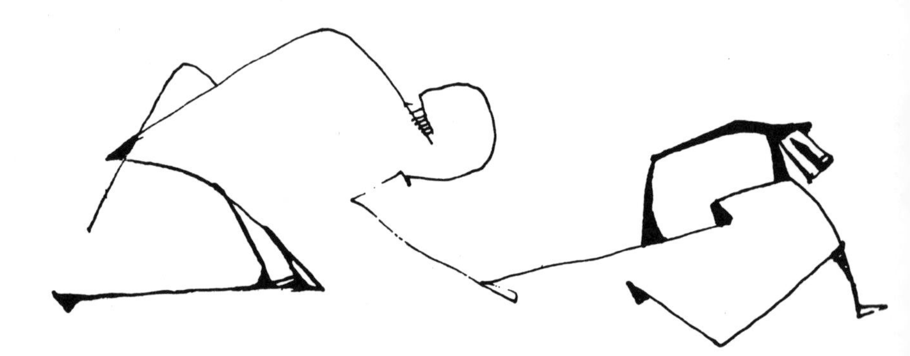

¡ay voz secreta del amor oscuro!
¡ay balido sin lanas! ¡ay herida!
¡ay aguja sin hiel, camelia hundida!
¡ay corriente sin mar, ciudad sin muro! . . .

Federico García Lorca

I

there's never been sunlight for this love
like a crazed flower it buds in the dark,
is at once a crown of thorns,
a spring garland around the temples

a fire, a wound, the most bitter fruit,
but a breeze as well, a source of water,
your breath—a bite to the soul,
your chest—a treetrunk in the current

make me walk on the turbid waters,
be the ax that breaks this lock,
the dew that weeps from trees

if I become mute kissing your thighs
it's that my heart eagerly
searches your flesh for a new dawn

I

para este amor nunca ha habido sol,
como loca flor, en lo oscuro brota,
es, a la vez, corona de espinas y
guirnalda de primavera en la sien

fuego, herida y amarguísimo fruto,
pero también brisa y manantial,
una mordida al alma: tu aliento,
un tronco en la corriente: tu pecho

hazme caminar sobre el agua turbia,
sé el hacha que rompa este candado,
el rocío que haga llorar los árboles

si mudo quedo al besar tus muslos
es que mi corazón con afán busca
entre tu carne un nuevo amanecer

II

your arms disarmed my sorrow,
by stretching like boughs
of elm in the night, they made
stars shine on the ceiling

we are no longer on the hard floor
of a poor apartment's living room,
nor do two quilts form our bed,
nor do we hide beneath covers

we are embracing on the warm earth,
night lulls us, very nearby
revealed, a river sings

I follow your voice as one follows
a torch in the dark mountainside,
far off, all are asleep in their bedrooms

II

tus brazos desarmaron mi tristeza,
bastó que se extendieran como ramas
de olmo por la noche para que luego
salieran las estrellas en el techo

ya no estamos en el macizo piso
de una sala de apartamento pobre,
ni forman nuestra cama dos colchas
encimadas, ni nos cubren cobijas

estamos abrazados a la tierra
cálida, la noche nos arrulla
descubierta, muy cerca canta un río

yo sigo tu voz como quien sigue
una antorcha en lo oscuro del monte
lejos, todos duermen en sus alcobas

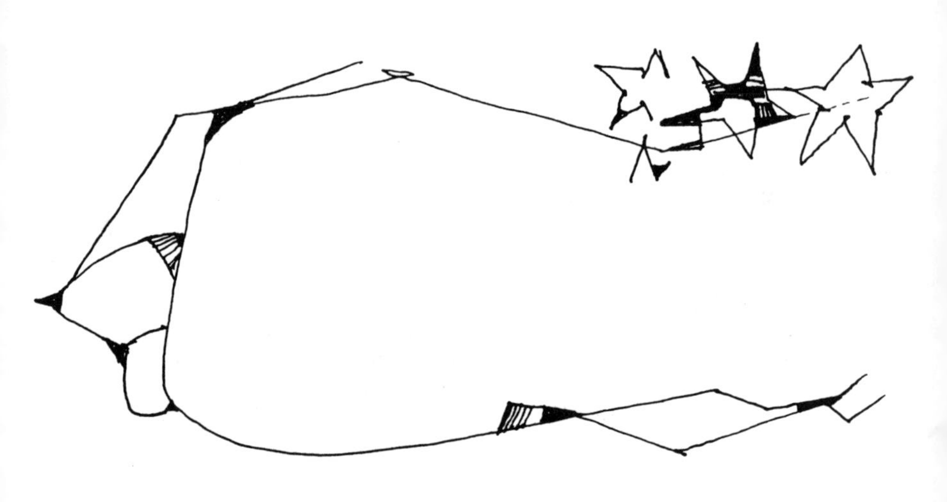

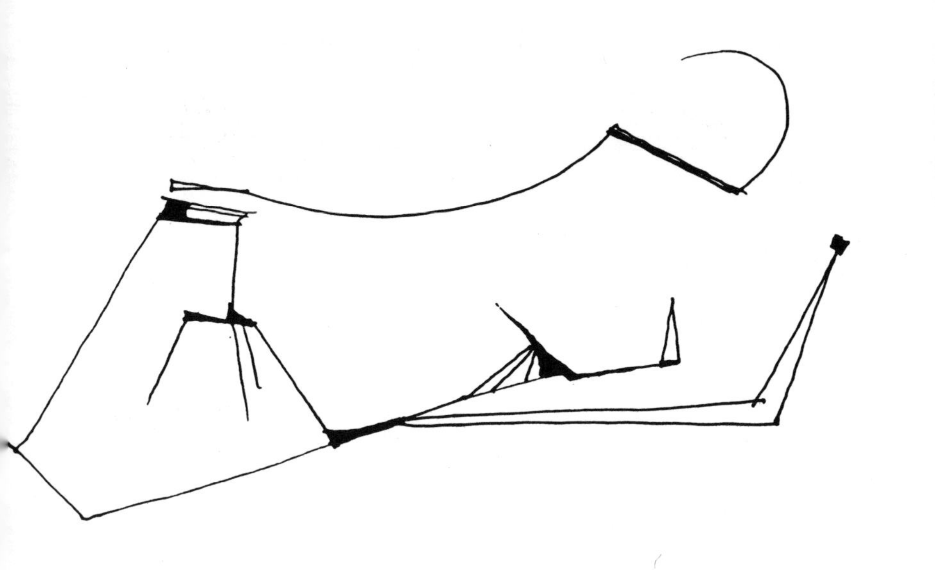

III

your voice is the lush murmur of an oasis,
I've been so thirsty so long,
I've forgotten the taste of words—
cool, tender, flowing from a spring

I listen, open the doors, the windows
of my being without reserve,
so that all my corners can enjoy
the health of your voice like fresh air

I am the shore that hoards your water,
my fields flourish simply at your sound,
you bring the freshness of humid moss

here you have me, dead with silence
lest I interrupt when you say:
"hey, Lazarus, rise and walk!"

III

tu voz es un murmullo verde de oasis,
yo he tenido tanta sed, tanto tiempo,
que ya no sé a qué saben las palabras
frescas, amorosas, de manantial

te escucho, abro las puertas, las ventanas
de mi ser de par en par, sin reservas,
para que todos mis rincones gocen
la salud de tu voz como del aire

yo soy la orilla que atesora tu agua,
mis campos reverdecen con sólo oírte,
tú traes la ternura del musgo húmedo

aquí me tienes muerto de silencio
para no interrumpirte cuando digas:
"¡eh, Lázaro, levántate y camina!"

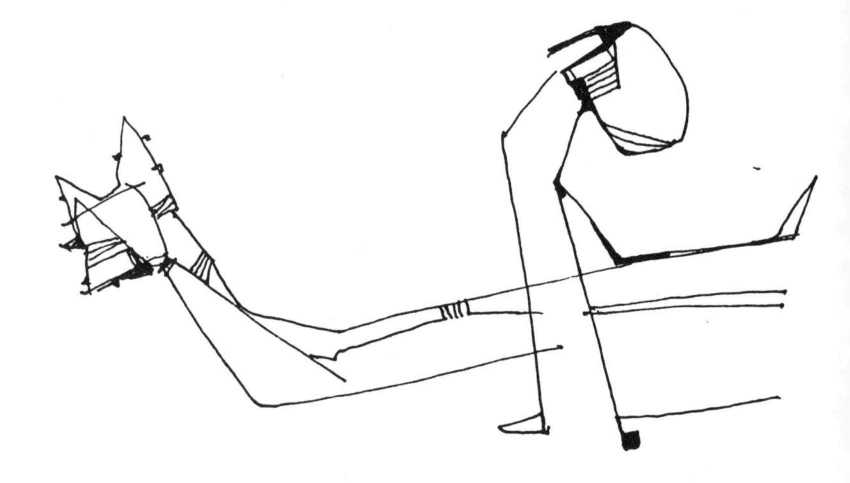

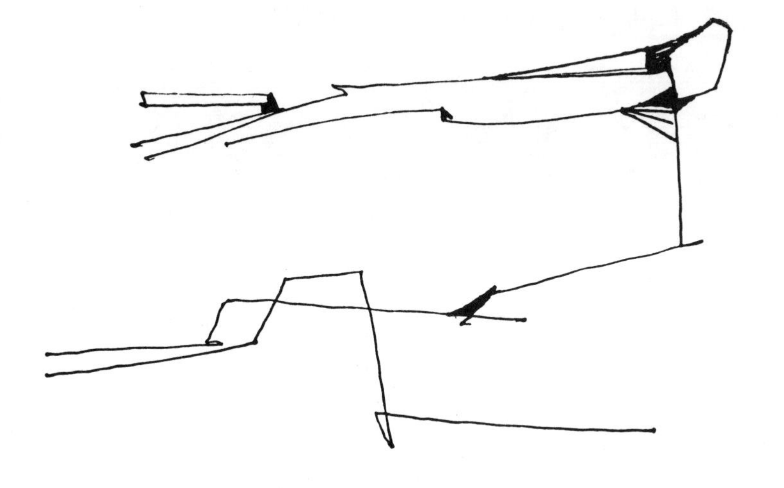

IV

your hands are two hammers that joyfully
nail down and pry up the morning,
tender fists that unfold from earth,
sweet bunches of small bananas

your hands smell of the blackberries
you harvest in the fields that steal
your sweat at two dollars a bucket,
they are hard, warm, young and wise

hoes that bring bread to the tables,
dark stones that give light when struck,
pleasure, support, anchor of the world

I worship them as reliquaries
because like nesting sea gulls,
they console, delight, defend me

IV

tus manos son dos martillos que clavan
y desclavan alegres la mañana,
tiernos puños desdoblados de tierra,
dulces pencas de plátanos pequeños

tus manos huelen a las zarzamoras
que cosechas en los campos que roban
tu sudor a dos dólares el bote,
son duras, tibias, jóvenes y sabias

azadones que traen pan a las mesas,
oscuras piedras que al chocar dan luz,
gozo, sostén, ancla del mundo entero

yo las venero como relicarios
porque como gaviotas anidadas,
me consuelan, me alegran, me defienden

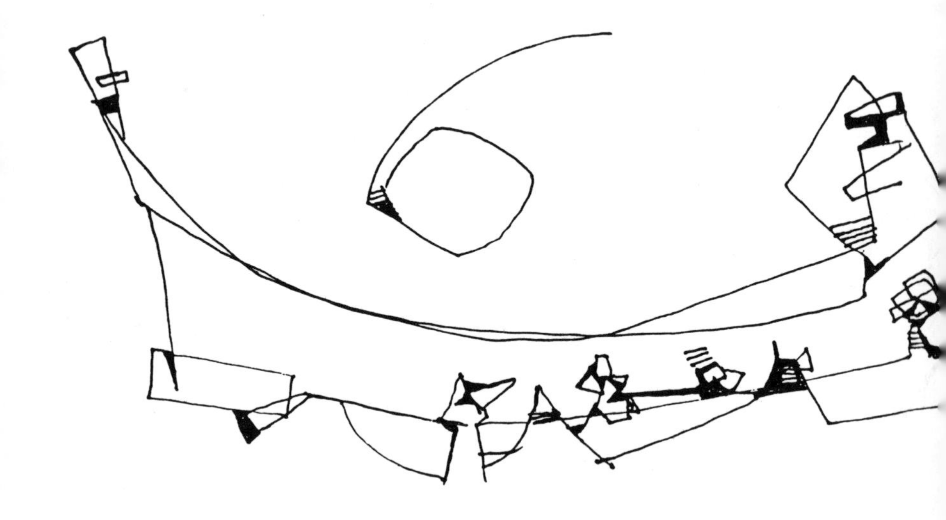

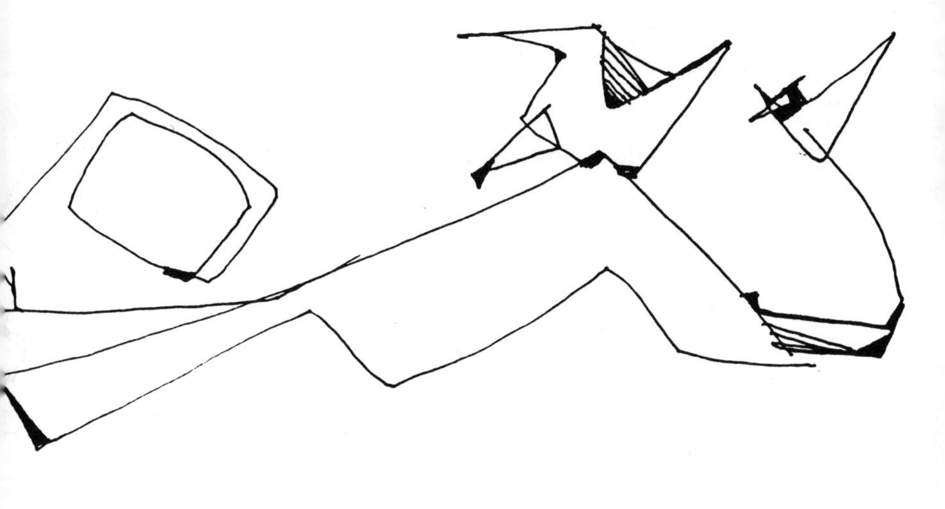

V

touching your shoulders blindly I touched
the cornerstone of every structure
in the universe: there, my boat ran aground,
there, my hands and my heels sank

the walls of my Jericho fell
at your feet like river sand,
and there, our armies surrendered
with a kiss before the first shot was fired

that was how our truce was sealed,
though I lost forever my calm,
letting my roofs burn free

night became day and I was filled
with ashes, recalling your chest
as one more wall of sorrow

V

en tus hombros sin ver toqué la piedra
angular de todas las construcciones
del universo, ahí encalló mi barca,
ahí se hundieron mis manos y talones

las murallas de mi Jericó cayeron
ante tus pies como arena del río,
ahí nuestros ejércitos se rindieron
con un beso antes del primer disparo

así quedó sellada nuestra tregua,
pero perdí para siempre la paz
al dejar que mis techos se incendiaran

la noche se hizo día y yo me llené
de cenizas memoriando tu pecho
como un muro más de lamentaciones

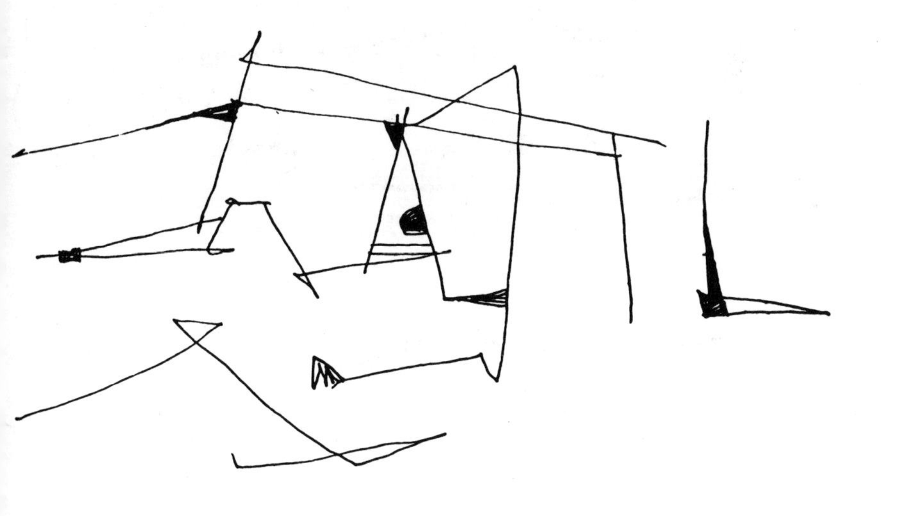

VI

asleep you become a continent—
long, mysterious, undiscovered,
the mountain ranges of your legs
encircle valleys and ravines

night slips past your eyelids,
your breath the swaying of the sea,
you stretch out so tenderly on the bed
like a dolphin beached on a shore

your mouth the mouth of a sated volcano,
o fragrant timber, what fire burns you?
you are so near, and yet so far

as you doze like a lily at my side,
I undo myself and invoke the moon:
now I am a dog guarding your sleep

VI

al dormir te vuelves un continente,
largo, misterioso, sin descubrir,
tus piernas: cordilleras apartadas,
van circundando valles y cañadas

la noche se resbala por tus párpados,
tu respirar: vaivén de olas de mar,
en la cama te extiendes mansamente
como un delfín alojado en la playa

tu boca: boca de volcán saciado,
leño perfumado, ¿en qué fuego ardes?
estás tan cercas y a la vez, tan lejos

mientras duermes como lirio a mi lado,
yo me deshago, invoco a la luna:
ahora soy el perro guardián de tu sueño

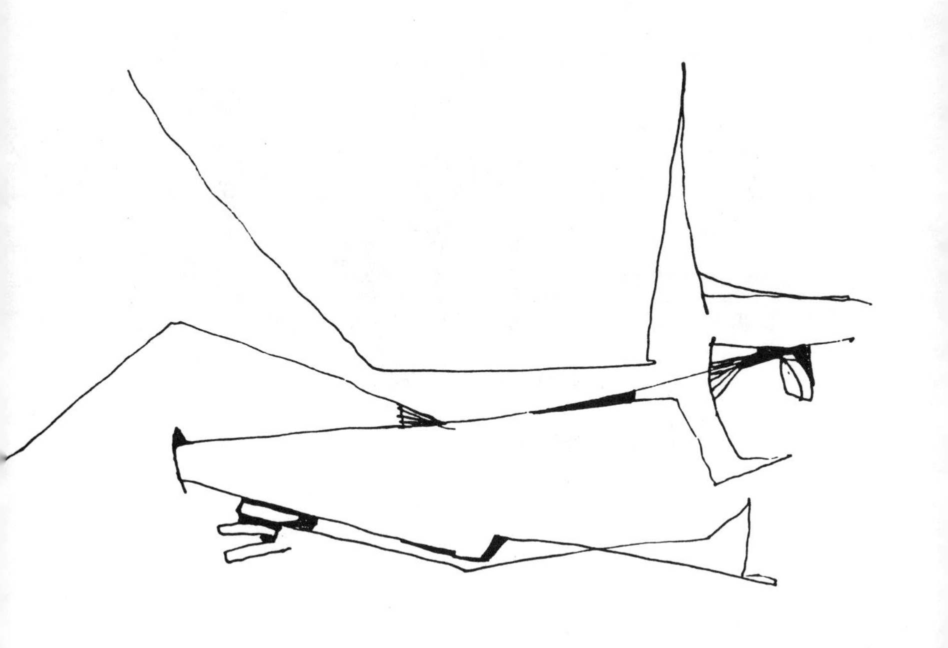

VII

I like to walk beside you, treading
your shadow along the way,
letting your steps mark my steps,
follow you like a boat being towed—

fitting my feet in the footprints
you leave like a puma on the sand,
I want to be the towel that dries you,
the one you spread to sunbathe

how lucky! the belt that gets to hug
your waist, the crucifix that hangs
from a chain on your chest!

what joy! to arrive every day as a comb
and smell the morning in your hair
but rather than comb, uncomb you!

VII

me gusta caminar junto a tu lado,
ir pisando en el malecón tu sombra,
dejar que tus pasos marquen mis pasos,
seguirte como barco remolcado

ajustando mis pies en las huellas
que como puma dejas en la playa,
quiero ser la toalla con que te secas,
donde te extiendes a tomar el sol

qué suerte la del cinturón que abraza
tu cintura, la del cristo que cuelga
de una cadena entre tus pectorales

qué alegría llegar como peine diario
a oler la mañana en tus cabellos
y en vez de peinarte, despeinarte

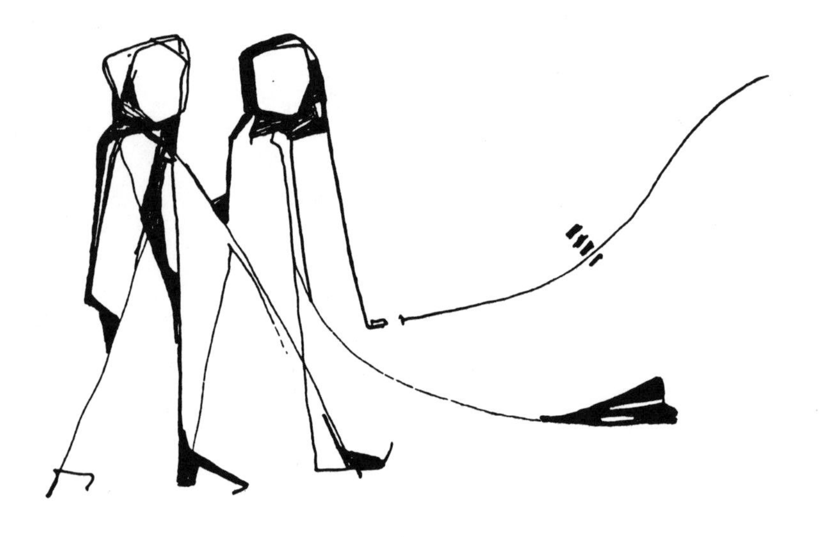

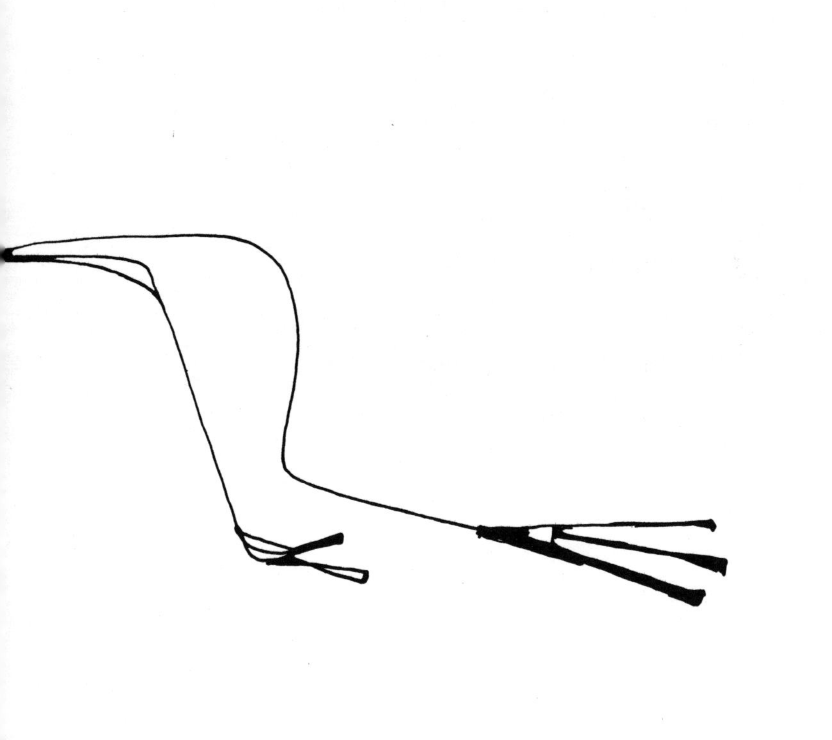

VIII

you gave me a basket of apples
sweet as the sweetness of your gaze,
as I bit them, they began to complain
about the sacks your back has handled,

and the ladders you've climbed
trying to pick the most beautiful—
those shining on the highest branches
of the apple trees at Summer's end

the apples are like your songs:
filled with water, morning, and sun,
cool as the laughter in your throat

juicy, fragrant, pissed, they clamor:
"we belong to those sweating foreheads,
those hands that picked and gathered us"

VIII

me diste una canasta de manzanas
tan dulces como tu dulce mirada
que al morder comenzaron a quejarse
por los sacos que ha cargado tu espalda

por las escalerillas que has subido
tratando de piscar las más hermosas,
las que brillan en las ramas más altas
de los manzanos al fin del verano

las manzanas son como tus canciones:
están llenas de agua, mañana y sol
frescas como la risa en tu garganta

jugosas, olorosas, enojadas
claman: "somos del sudor de la frente
y de las manos que nos cosecharon"

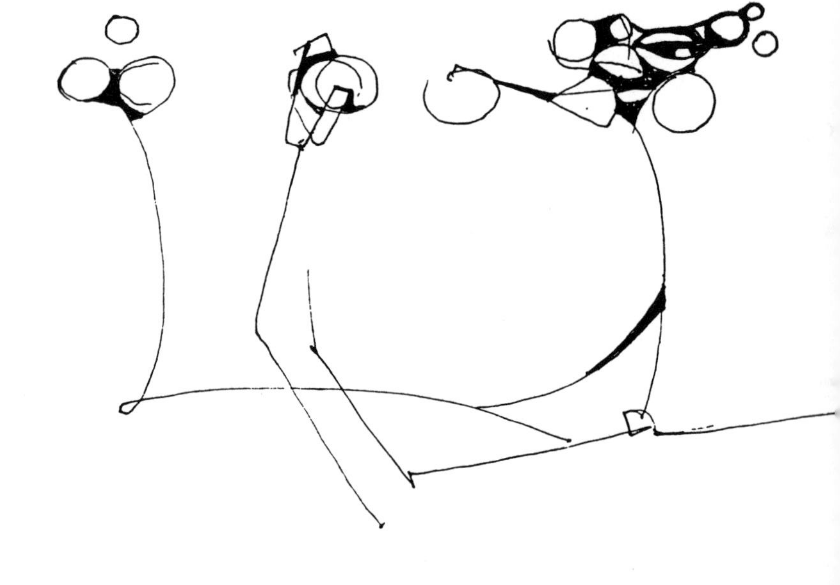

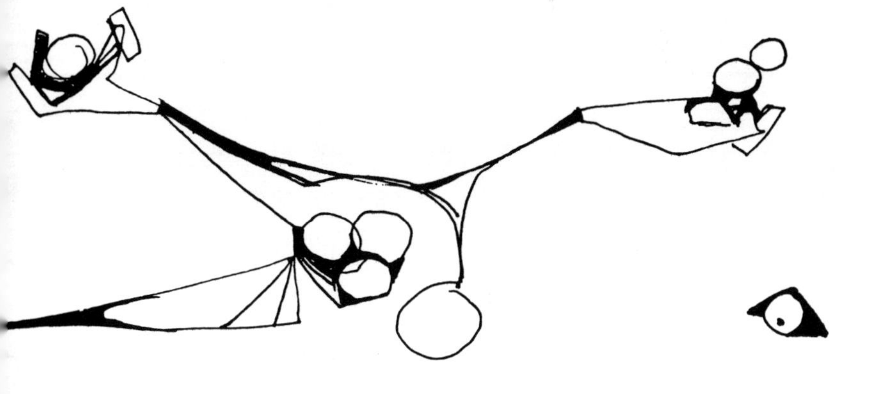

IX

I woke sad and silent, overcast,
and though it isn't raining,
the ache of a hurricane whirls
inside me, water overflowing my roofs

I toss the sky and day at this torrent,
the bars of this cage drip blood
of a crazed bird, what wings
could lift such a heavy heart?

the shouts, prayers, insults and sobs
within the walls of this madhouse
would cease if you'd only call

I haven't seen you, you haven't called
in days: I am on the gallows, the phone
is becoming my somber guillotine

IX

amanecí mudo y triste, sin sol,
y aunque en esta temporada no llueva,
yo lluevo por dentro un dolor ciclón,
llevo inundadas hasta las azoteas

a la torrente arrojo cielo y día,
las barras de esta jaula escurren sangre
de pájaro enloquecido, ¿qué alas
pueden con tan pesado corazón?

hay gritos, rezos, injurias, lloriqueos
tras los postigos de este manicomio
que una llamada tuya cerraría

hace días que no te veo ni tú me hablas,
estoy en un cadalso, comienzo a ver
como guillotina gris al teléfono

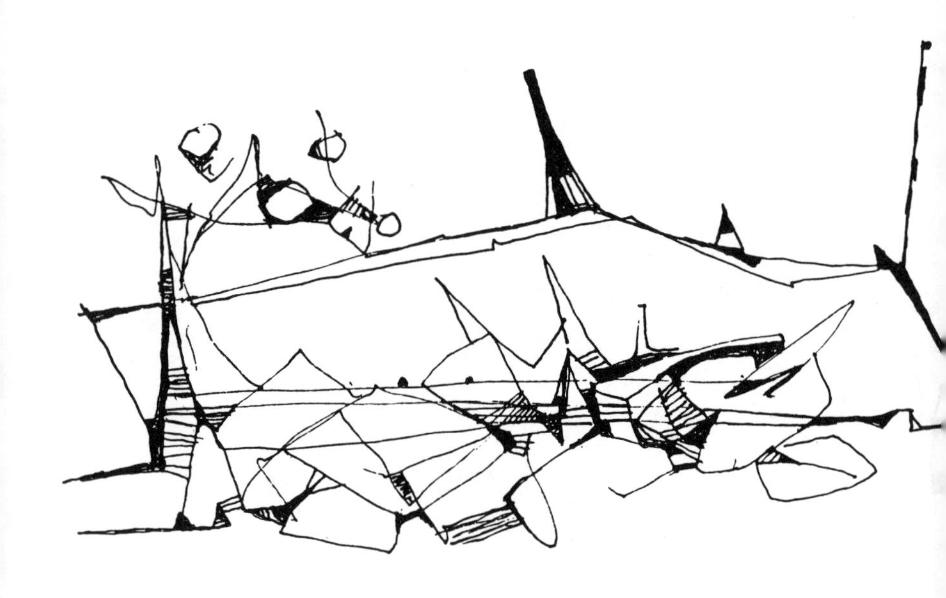

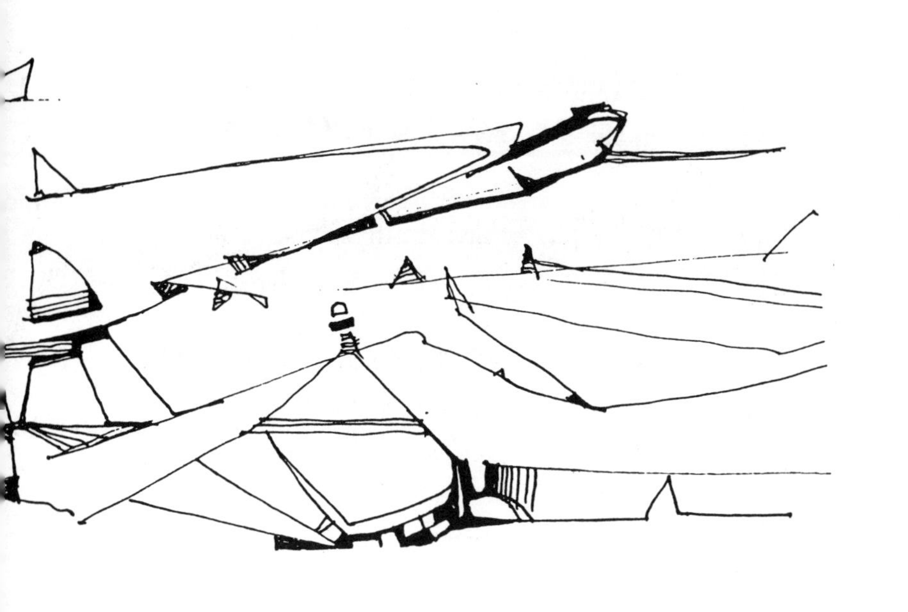

X

"There are two ways in the world: to see
yourself one day in the mirror, or never see
your true self-image, to see yourself is to live,
not seeing yourself is death," you tell me

"look at me, I am more than my look,
more than a passing smile on a street,
more than piled horizons, the one who looks
at you is more than the one you look at"

"seeing myself in you, I discover who I am,
I want you to see yourself likewise in me:
looking at me, see yourself looking at you"

"look at me, for I see myself in you,
look at me, for you are my mirror,
look at me, I want to be yours"

X

"dos caminos hay en el mundo: el verse
un día en un espejo o el nunca llegar
a verse de veras, verse es vivir,
no verse, estar muerto," me aleccionas

"mírame, yo soy más que mi mirada,
más que una sonrisa en plena calle,
más que todos los horizontes juntos:
el que te mira es más que ése que miras"

"al verme en ti, descubro lo que soy,
así quiero que tú te veas en mí:
que al mirame te mires mirándote"

"mírame que me estoy mirando en ti,
mírame que tú eres espejo mío
mírame que yo quiero ser el tuyo"

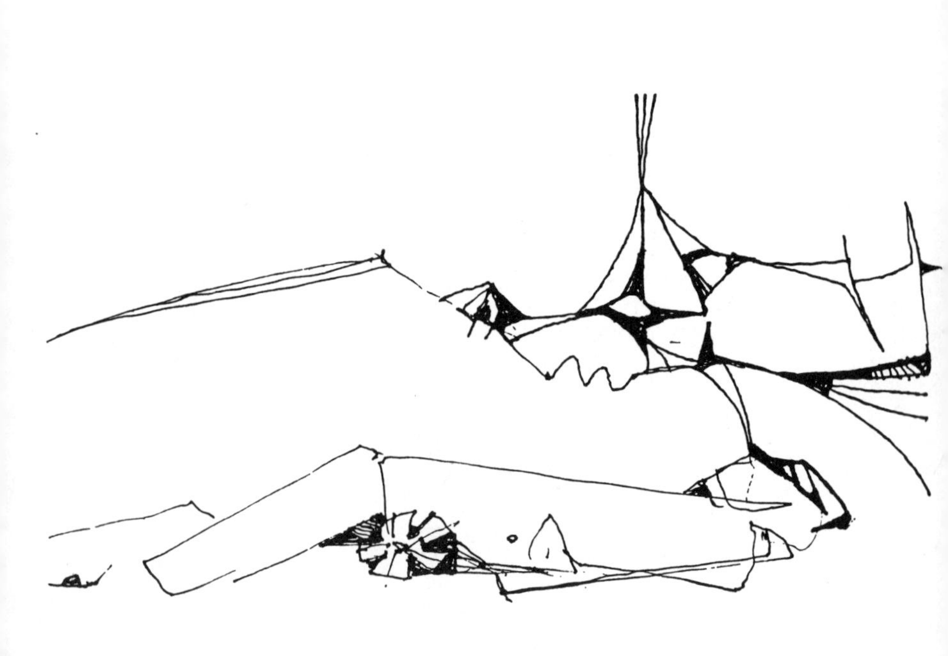

XI

since I met you on the road,
I am no longer the same, a blind man
no more, tripping on his own shadow,
I am no longer deaf to landscapes

to follow you swiftly I've tossed aside
my cross, rid myself of those violins
always playing soap opera tunes,
I no longer walk, I run barefoot

ever since I heard the rumor of your voice,
all other words ring hollow to me—
useless, cumbersome, bewitching

this is why I no longer want to write poems
but live them with you: embers
blazing in a fire outside language

XI

desde que te conocí en el camino,
yo ya no soy el mismo, ya no soy el ciego
que se tropieza con su propia sombra,
ya no soy el sordo que no oye el paisaje

para seguirte ligero he tirado
mi cruz, he despedido a los violines
que siempre me tocaban melodramas,
ya no ando, corro con los pies descalzos

desde que escuché el rumor de tu voz,
las demás palabras se me hacen huecas,
inútiles, estorbosas, hechizas

por eso ya no quiero escribir poemas
sino vivirlos contigo: que sean
brasas de un fuego fuera del lenguaje

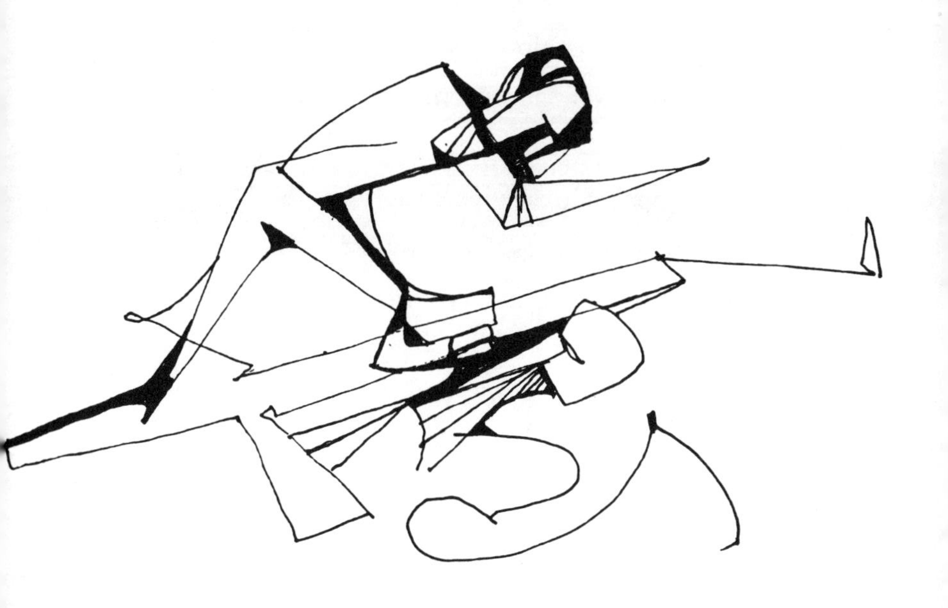

XII

once again I look out your window
and the world looks oddly different,
maybe the fields have blossomed,
or, perhaps, more stars have been born

delirious waves caress my feet,
something new, unknown,
sunsets whisper in my ear as well,
everywhere, I find your odor, your shape

you are among old growth pines,
in the fog along the coastal rocks,
around the most somber of afternoons

impossible to wipe away your joy
from my eyes, from my sad mouth:
you are the universe made flesh

XII

por tu ventana me asomo otra vez
al mundo que algo tiene diferente,
quizás hayan florecido los campos,
o tal vez hayan nacido más estrellas

las olas me acarician, delirantes,
los pies, algo nuevo, desconocido,
me susurran también los crepúsculos,
en todo hallo tu aroma, tu figura

tú estás entre los pinos milenarios,
tras la neblina en las peñas marinas,
en medio de la tarde más sombría

imposible borrar tu regocijo
de mis ojos, de mi triste boca,
así eres: el universo hecho carne

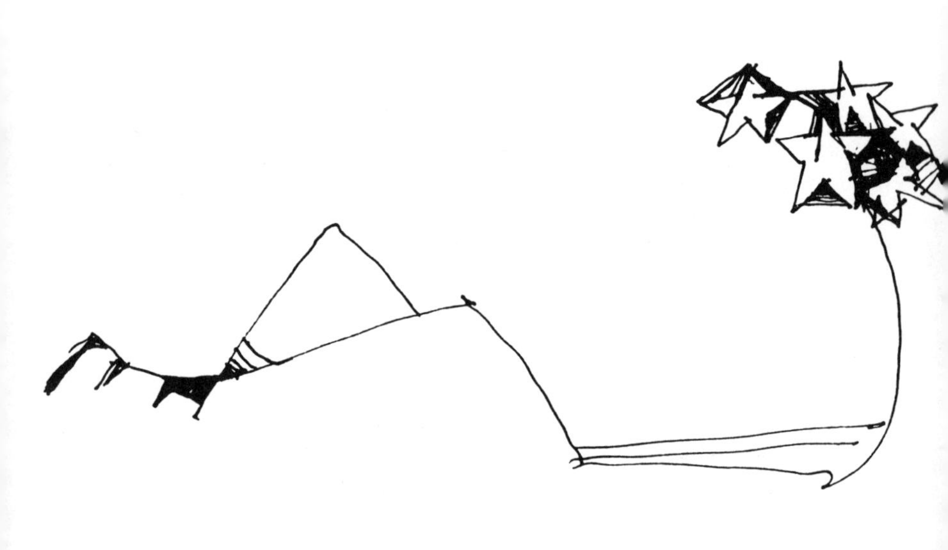

XIII

o body, where have you fled from me—
on what night, on what corner, in what hall?
why didn't you tell me, or leave a note?
do you hate me? have I made you suffer so?

some days I'd take you for a stroll,
we'd go to the park or the beach—
wasn't that your joy? you'd play
in the water like a child, remember?

o body of mine, such an orphan of love,
I'm haunted by everything I denied you,
now I'd like to kiss you to the bone

I find you walking alone on the street,
your shoes are untied, come, body:
yes, I accept you, stop crying

XIII

¿en dónde te me has escapado cuerpo,
en qué noche, en qué esquina, en qué atrio?
¿por qué no me diste aviso o una nota?
¿tanto me odias? ¿así te he hecho sufrir?

a veces yo te sacaba a pasear,
juntos íbamos al parque o a la playa,
¿no era ése tu antojo? tú te bañabas
de gusto como niño, ¿no te acuerdas?

ay, cuerpo mío, tan huérfano de amor,
cómo me duele haberte negado tanto,
ahora quisiera besarte hasta el hueso

te hallo caminando solo en la calle,
llevas desamarrados los zapatos,
ven cuerpo: sí, te acepto, ya no llores

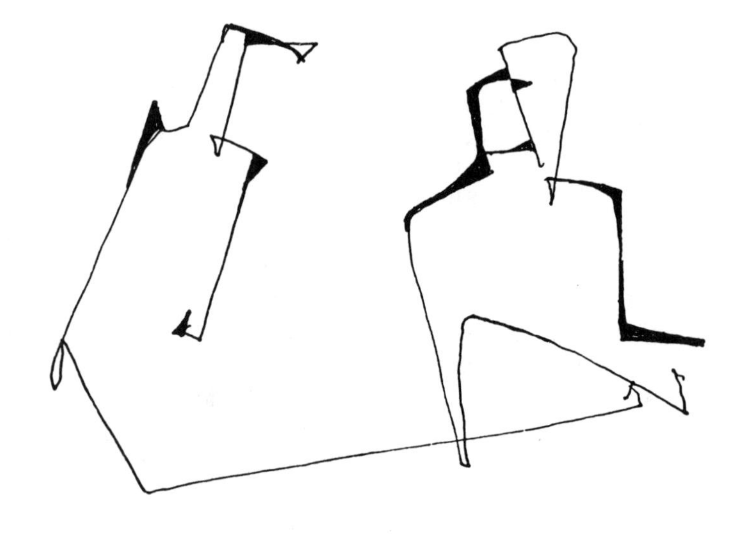

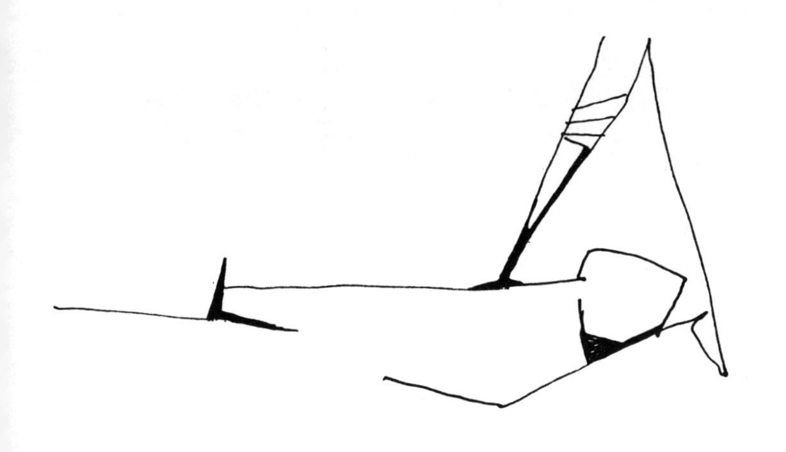

XIV

how to console the loneliest man
on earth? how to relieve his pain?
how to call through his bolted door
and have one's soul speak to his ear:

"brother, the war is now over:
all of us in the end emerged victors:
go forth and enjoy the liberated fields:
exploitation is a thing of the past"?

what to do when he returns, wounded
with barbed wire between his legs?
how to face his eyes accusing:

"brother, it's business as usual in the world:
we the poor are still easy prey: love,
if isn't for everyone, it isn't enough"?

XIV

¿cómo consolar al hombre más solo
de la tierra? ¿cómo aliviar su pena?
¿cómo llamar a su puerta atrancada
y decirle al oído embocado de alma:

"hermano, la guerra ya ha terminado:
todos, por fin, salimos vencedores:
sal, goza los campos liberados:
la explotación es cosa del pasado"?

¿qué hacer cuando regrese malherido
con alambre de púas entre las piernas?
¿cómo encarar sus ojos que denuncian:

"hermano, el mundo sigue igual:
los pobres todavía somos presa fácil:
el amor, si no es de todos, no basta"?

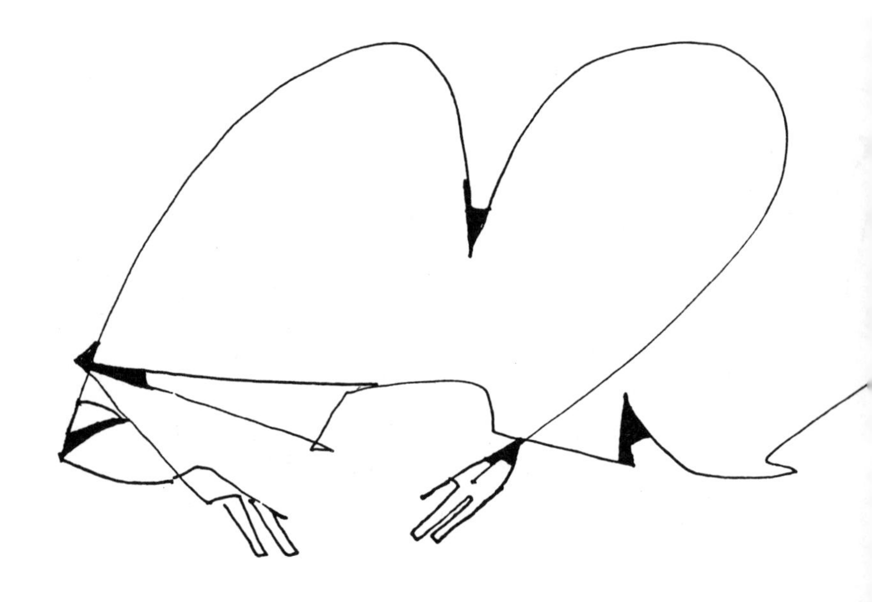

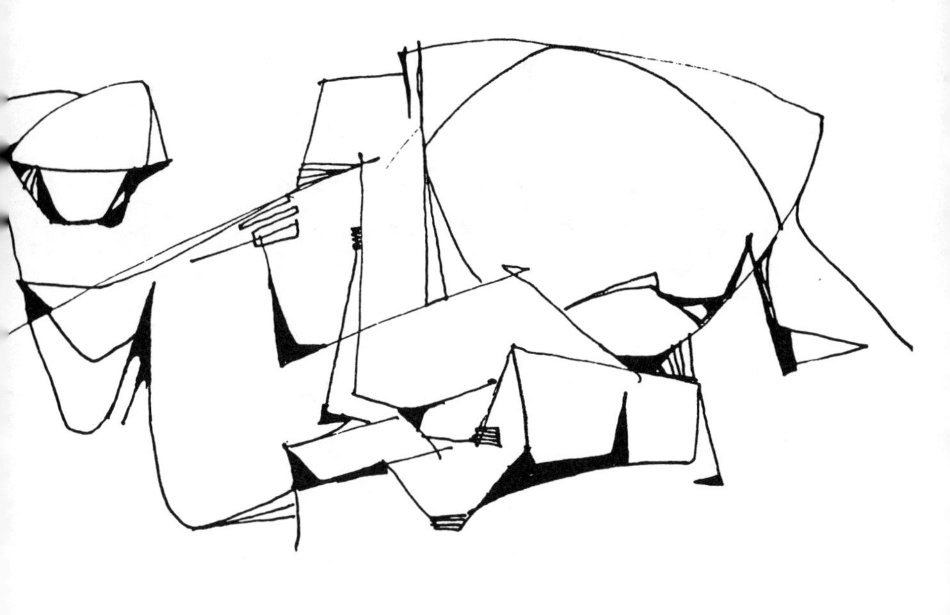

Photo by Francisco Dominguez

FRANCISCO X. ALARCÓN, Chicano poet and educator, was born in Los Angeles, grew up in Guadalajara, Mexico, is the author of nine volumes of poetry, including *Body in Flames/Cuerpo en llamas* (Chronicle Books, 1990), *Snake Poems: An Aztec Invocation* (Chronicle Books, 1992), and *No Golden Gate for Us* (Pennywhistle Press, 1993). His books of bilingual poetry for children, *Laughing Tomatoes and Other Spring Poems* (Children's Book Press, 1997) and *From the Bellybutton of the Moon and Other Summer Poems* (Children's Book Press, 1998) both won the Pura Belpré Honor Award from the American Library Association in 1997 and 2000. His other honors include a Fulbright Fellowship, the Before Columbus Foundation American Book Award, the Pen Oakland Josephine Miles Award, and the UC Irvine Chicano Literary Prize. He currently teaches at the University of California, Davis, where he directs the Spanish for Native Speakers Program.

* * *

A native of San Francisco and former editor of *The Berkeley Poetry Review*, **FRANCISCO ARAGON** is the author of the chapbook, *Light, Yogurt, Strawberry Milk.* His translations have appeared in various journals, including *Chelsea*, *Luna*, *Quarry West* and *Poetry Flash.* He received his MA in English from UC Davis, where he was awarded an Academy of American Poets Prize in 1999. A long-time resident of Spain, his work appears in anthologies: *American Diaspora: Poetry of Exile* (University of Iowa Press, 2000) and *Inventions of Farewell* (Norton, 2001). He is finishing his first full-length collection of poems, a bilingual volume whose working title is *Puerta del Sol.*

Originally designed and printed by Felicia Rice with Scott Fields in an edition of seventy copies on Frankfurt Cream paper using Janson types; pen and ink drawings printed from photopolymer plates made by Eric Holub; bound in Iris book cloth over boards by BookLab: ISBN 0-939952-09-2. In addition seven hundred copies were printed offset by Jeff Kissell and perfect bound: ISBN 0-939952-08-4; © 1991 by Francisco X. Alarcón. Second offset edition published with a library binding: ISBN 0-939952-15-7; © 1992 by Francisco X. Alarcón. Thanks to Maureen Carey and to the California Arts Council for their support. Third offset edition: ISBN 0-939952-23-8; © 2001 by Francisco X. Alarcón.

Moving Parts Press
10699 Empire Grade
Santa Cruz, California 95060
(831) 427-2271
www.movingpartspress.com

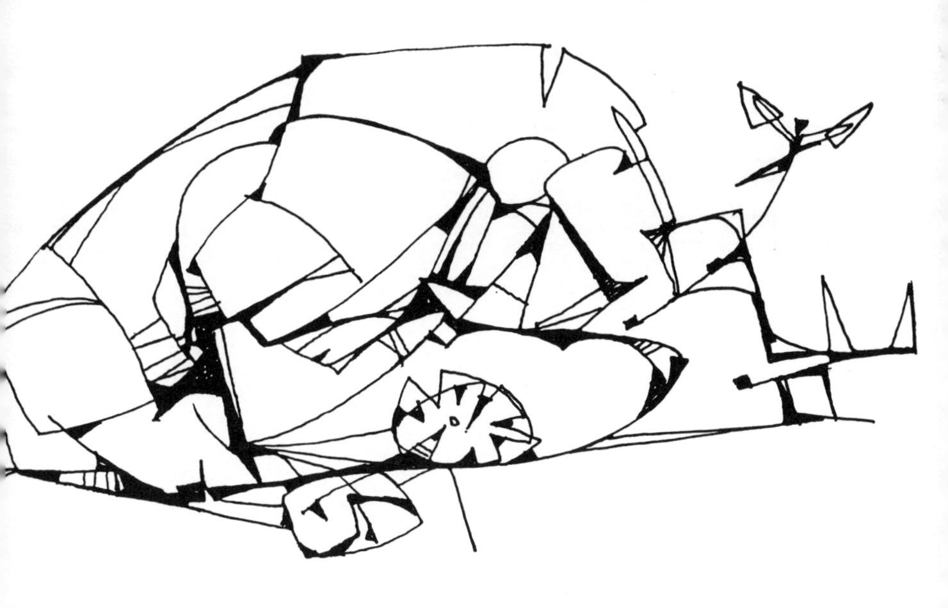